Ken Weir was born in Ireland during the Second World War. He went to school in England (Oundle), got his BA at Oxford (Pembroke College), and his medical degrees (BM. BCh. and DM) were also from Oxford. His clinical training in cardiology was at the Groote Schuur hospital in Cape Town, South Africa, where he and his wife, Elizabeth V. Pearman, first met. His research training was at the CVP Lab of the University of Colorado in Denver, as a Fulbright scholar. His clinical, research, and teaching careers have been at the Minneapolis VA Medical Center and the University of Minnesota Medical School. He has edited 11 scientific books and is an author of over 200 scientific papers but these poems, which have been written in the Twin Cities over the last twenty years, are his first volume of poetry.

This collection of poems is written for my muse, mentor, wife, Liz (Moom), who has taught me much of what I know about poetry and without whom, nothing (our sons, Fergus and Conor included), would have been conceived. I am also very grateful to our friends, especially Seth Hoyt, John Wheelihan, and Mary Pike (+ Fergus and Conor), for reading the poems and for making suggestions. I greatly appreciate the work of Stefan Iwaskewycz, whose photography of my bronze statues illustrate the book (FotoStefan on Facebook).

Ken Weir Pembroke '61.

WHAT DO YOU THINK?

weirx002@umn.edu

AUSTIN MACAULEY PUBLISHERS™
LONDON • CAMBRIDGE • NEW YORK • SHARJAH

Ordering Information
Quantity sales: Special discounts are available on quantity purchases by corporations, associations, and others. For details, contact the publisher at the address below.

Publisher's Cataloguing-in-Publication data
Weir, Ken
What Do You Think?

ISBN 9798886935349 (Paperback)
ISBN 9798886935356 (ePub e-book)

Library of Congress Control Number: 2023917698

www.austinmacauley.com/us

First Published 2023
Austin Macauley Publishers LLC
40 Wall Street, 33rd Floor, Suite 3302
New York, NY 10005
USA

mail-usa@austinmacauley.com
+1 (646) 5125767

Table of Contents

Introduction

As a physician, I frequently have to search for a diagnosis which will account for most, or hopefully all, of a patient's problems. So when I consider a question related to politics, religion or philosophy, I look for an answer that will help us to understand the known facts. A pleasure of poetry is that it allows us to distil an idea down to its essentials, to express a concept in a few words. "Poetic license" gives us permission to explore a thought which is not often discussed. When you read these poems, I don't expect that you will necessarily agree with the conclusions but hope that you will be stimulated to ask, "What do I think?" and, maybe of more importance, "Why do I think so?" The interpretations will be a product of age, gender, culture, race, nationality, politics, education and religious beliefs, or lack of them. It is hardly surprising that our responses may differ. I frequently apply the following quotation from Oliver Cromwell (1599-1650), the Lord Protector of England, Scotland and Ireland, to my own thoughts: "I beseech you, in the bowels of Christ, think it possible you may be mistaken." Letter to the General Assembly of the Church of Scotland (8/3/1650).

Modern poets often feel that the reader should earn their understanding of a poem. As a scientist, I would rather try to make the meaning clear. Most would agree that it is helpful to know the context in which a poem was written. Consequently, for many of these poems, I have added a short footnote to provide background information. I grew up in Ireland, just South of Dublin, so elements of my Irish heritage are reflected in some of the writing. The poems included in this volume cover many topics; science, politics, medicine, religion, age, love, death, and humor.

Several of my bronze sculptures illustrate a few of the poems.

Section 1

Transience

This section may be best introduced by a few lines from Shakespeare's *Macbeth* (1605) Act III, scene 1, line 113
"Out, out, brief candle!
Life's but a walking shadow,
A poor player that struts and frets his hour upon the stage,
and then is heard no more."

Twilight

Death roosts in an old winter ash,
aware of every furtive dash.
On windless days we sense him there,
as silent wings caress the air.

But at the end, we hear no call,
just sudden weight and sudden fall.
We go as all wild creatures must,
prey to predator and dust to dust.

Sursum Corda

Transplantation is Transubstantiation,
leveraging the depths of despair
into the gift of life and hope,
transforming Good Friday into Easter.

This is the Body and Blood of another,
life signifies death and joy springs from tears.
Lazarus does not walk from the tomb
unless another enters. Gratias agimus.

Anna (22 years), the daughter of a close neighbor, received a heart transplant on Easter morning.

Sursum corda: Lift up your hearts.
Gratias agimus: We give thanks.
Words of the Latin mass

The Shards of Time

The dinosaur that stands fossilized
upon my desk, ran on the earth
200 million years ago.
In the terrain of papers and pens,
she is reunited with
the ammonites and trilobites

that populated her world.
Homo sapiens, a species
a thousand-fold younger,
now steers the ark.
On whose desk will we rest
a million years hence?

Written contemplating the fossil of a small dinosaur found in China.

Out of Africa

We ventured out of Africa
a hundred millennia past,

crossed the Red Sea together
with Moses and the Israelites,

festered in slave ships across the
careless unknown of the Atlantic.

We push North in dinghies to seek
success beyond the Mediterranean.

The spark of life that kindled there
now burns throughout the world.

We are all the sons and daughters of Africa.

Youth

You hold it so lightly,
each month, each year,
a trifle.

Oblivious of the time
when each minute is heavy
and worthless
as gold.

When I Die

I return to the earth quietly:
no thunder, no comets in the sky,
no sound or sight of soul ascending.
I die as Homo sapiens over 300,000 years
and hominids for millions more;
not Christian, Muslim, Hindu or Buddhist
but revering the sun, fearing the moon,
terrified of the dark, the starless night.
I return to nature, as every other
animal that runs its course.

Was It for This?

Eyes open.
Rorschach blot.
Life is such a blast.
Focus on delight.
New light, new love, new life.
Deadlines, dead hopes, deadbeat.
Less time, no time.
No time like the past.
Lifetime, lost time.
Eyes close.

A "Rorschach blot" is a random splatter of ink on a page, used by psychologists to stimulate spontaneous responses and free association of ideas.

Beyond Bolero

From the last breath draw life.
Breath begets breath and breath, pulse.
Back from the brink to staggered gait,
back to pain and fractured sight.
Old friends return across the Styx,
return to misremember memories,
to cold nights of memories alone.
Grieving alone, single alone, bereaved alone.
Days of shared parting, nights of dread.
Afternoons, books, travel, and teas together,
warm still evenings precede early risings,
early risings presage years of fruitless work.
Earlier risings engender sons,
sons and lovers, lovers of sons,
lovers of license.
First love, unloved,
unsure, unsteady,
wrapped, warm,
pulse again,
beat again.
Life begins
with an
orgasm.

Those who love Ravel's Bolero will recognize the slow start, increasing tempo and tempestuous climax, even if not, perhaps, the reversed order of life.

Transience

Love, like autumn leaves, is transient,
it flares, fades, and falls,
through death, dementia, and deceit.
I, like Orpheus, am left at Hades' door
holding your crumpled coat.

Waking Alone

The pain returned at three,
hands stretch out
but feel no warmth,
eyes open wide
but sense no light.

As the sentry for the dawn,
as the salmon for the fly,
as the surfer for the wave,
even so do I,
I yearn for death.

Charon's Game

There are too many in this tug-of-war
and every day their strength grows more.
Our bravest and our best are gone.
Some struggled in the tide,
some slipped below the wave,
some never knew the rope was taut
until the other side.
We cross them off our team,
Chris, Alan, Terri gone,
the friends who fought to live.
We weary of this strife,
our eyes are dim, our arms grow tired,
our hearts cry out, "enough".
But then, fresh hope appears.
Another cry, a cry of life;
new players join the game,
Sophadevy,
Satyamuni,
Sorika,
Sivanna.
We cannot fail to win.

Chris, Alan, and Terri were friends and colleagues who died too young. Our grandchildren are the new players. Charon is the boatman ferrying souls across the river Styx.

Ragtime

Delivered on the same day,
identical in every fiber,
cosseted among sheets and towels,
sharing life's vicissitudes,
we were inseparable.

In wind and sunshine
we danced together,
toe to identical toe,
until in the maelstrom
we were torn apart.

Now, down at heel,
tumbled in the embrace of strangers,
each is known only to the other
by a hole worn in the threadbare sole.

Conceit

We stand on this planet,
one amongst billions,
as sand on the shore,
innumerable.
Beyond the nearest star
the universe expands
through millions of light years.

For 300,000 years
(the flare of a match),
Homo sapiens imagined
we came from the Sun,
from Mount Olympus,
or a personal God,
who listens to our every plea.

Prosaic as it may be,
we emerged from the sea
and return to the earth.

Death, Be Not Proud

With only a few leaves still defying the October winds, Death comes as a timely caller. Her visits have become more frequent of recent years, her invitations less implausible.

In youth, the Fall carried the kernel promise of Spring; squirrels hid their store, the surety that they would emerge when the snows had gone. The aged cannot see beyond the snow.

Death is not an unwelcome guest, just a more persistent, older rendering of the enticing woman who briefly touched your arm in younger years. Maybe today you will walk with her awhile, maybe tomorrow hold her hand. For now you may resist her charms, deny her allure but, as certain as Winter's grip, she will have you.

The title, "Death Be Not Proud", is from a sonnet by John Donne
(1571–1631): Holy Sonnet 10

No Reason

Since my brother died
I fear no death.
Those who are blind
can gaze at the sun.
Since my mother died
I lost my soul.
The motherless
seek no salvation.
Since my father died
I lost my reason.
Since my child lives
I have no reason,
no reason to die.

Inheritance

In 1858 great-grandfather
found and ploughed the land,
corralled the cattle and
brought his bride to this fair Eden.

The farm lay in a hanging valley;
a lake, fed from the snow above,
gave water to the home and
woods provided winter warmth.

Grandpa's family flourished; the trees
gave way to fields and chapel,
the dirt path paved and wells were dug,
safeguard against the summer drought.

Where Dad once caught the large-mouth bass,
a fish-farm feeds the many mouths below
but now the woods are gone, spring floods,
erode the land and in the Fall, the harvest fails.

Cousin feuds with cousin to tap the dying stream
but still are we blessed with many babies
and trust that Providence will provide,
so we can remain, stewards of His land.

Reflections of a Jellyfish

My ancestors took a billion years
to evolve into those folk but they only took
the last few hundred to achieve extinction.

As the Earth turns and burns
within its darkening shroud,
the glaciers melt, the coasts recede
beneath the flooding tide and
the hills shrivel in drought.

Maybe we can do better
next time.

Breakfast Time

The editorials are benign.
Juncos forage in the snow,
below the brimming feeder.
A hairy woodpecker pecks
staccato on the oak.
A Cooper's hawk plunges down,
feathers drift across
my window; time to read
the obituaries.

Three Hundred Millennia

Relentlessly the clock
pursues us all,
until tick reaches tock
and we fall.
Tide by tide,
season by season,
the generations surge
further up the beach,
oblivious to reason.

The human tsunami
inundates the land.
The Earth owes us
nothing. It was here
through billions of years
before we appeared
and will remain,
long after we return
to the sand.

Three Score Years and Ten

Clicking and grinding of joints
are early signs of trouble.
Hip replacement is followed
by dental crowns, cataract
surgery and valve repair.
Hearing migrates to a shell
in the ear and the pace
of the pulse is determined
not by the lust of a lover
but by a box wired to the heart.
Central control loses access
to the memory banks and,
before long, you reach
your second infancy.

"The days of our years are threescore years and ten."
Psalm 90:10

The Sculpture “Sans Eyes, Sans Teeth, Sans Taste, Sans Everything”

William Shakespeare: *As You Like It*; Act 2, Scene 7

Section 2

Medicine and Science

"It is in knowledge that man has found his greatness and his happiness."
James Smithson (died 1829).

"It doesn't require many words to speak the truth."
Chief Joseph (died 1904).

"The test of a first-rate intelligence is the ability to hold two opposed ideas in the mind at the same time, and still retain the ability to function."
F. Scott Fitzgerald (died 1940).

Right Brain, Left Brain

The artistic mind is quickly lost,
teasing words to phrase a thought,
seeing shapes in scattered frost,
hearing voices in the rain.

The scientific mind is
precisely
focused only on
the matter at
hand.

This may lead to mingling of the sharp and yellow.

Better termed cognitive dissonance.

Or to fusion of the coarse and mellow.

Self-indulgent neurotic.

Differential Diagnosis

The boots still showed
the dirt of South Dakota.
The gravel in his voice
sprang from that soil.

“It hurts here.” A finger
pointed center shirt.
“Exercise, Doc? Not much
except Bull Poker.

Bull Poker? A hundred dollars
on the forehead of the bull;
him with the fastest feet,
quickest grab, gets the dough.

No. There’s no pain when
I ride the bull, though
I’m hells focused then.
Nitro? No nitro, just vodka neat.

No heart problem? Thanks, Doc
but why the pain?
Oh, no, not the drink.
The day I quit, I quit the game."

This patient with chest pain was referred for consideration of a coronary angiogram. However, chest pain which was not provoked by strenuous exercise, such as "Bull Poker", was unlikely to be angina and was probably caused by esophageal inflammation related to his vodka consumption.
Nitro is nitroglycerine, given for the relief of angina.
The poem has been previously published in the Minnesota Medical Journal.

The Ancient Cath Lab Tech (after Samuel Coleridge)

It is an ancient Cath Lab Tech
and he stoppeth one of three.
"By thy long beard and glittering eye
now wherefore stopp'st thou me?"

"The cath lab doors are opened wide
and I am next to scrub;
the patient's prepped, the table's made;
may'st hear the fierce *hubbub*."

He holds him with his glittering eye—
the cardiologist stood still.
and listens like a three years' child;
the Cath Tech hath his will.

The sheath was placed, the vessel clear,
swiftly did we march,
beyond the spine, beyond the gut,
beyond the aortic arch.

The blood came up upon the left,
out of the valve came he,
and he flowed bright and, on the right,
went down to the mesentery.

The coronary vessels did show up
but were there lesions there?
With much to lose and many views
the cardiologist tore his hair.

And now there came the IVUS
and it grew wondrous dark
and plaque so high, came floating by,
as thick as elm bark.

And through the blood the pearly plaque
did send a dismal sheen:
nor shapes of branch or bend he ken—
the fog was all between.

T'was five o'clock on the weekend
and all were loathe to serve
but the cardiologist demanded
a fractional flow reserve.

"God save thee, ancient Cath Lab Tech,
from the fiends that so persist!
Why look'st thou so?"—"With my cam'ra,
I crushed the cardiologist."

IVUS: Intra-vascular ultrasound

For J T R

The sun rose in Hazard.
For many years he towered in our sky,
warm, strong and nurturing,
sometimes fierce and scorching.
Uncompromising,
like an Old Testament prophet,
his passion etched in the lives of others.

Now, suddenly, the light is gone
as when the sun drops behind the Colorado Rockies.
But his warmth stays in our hearts
and the light which burned in his eyes
must shine in ours.

John T Reeves MD. "Jack," was born in Hazard, Kentucky, 17th November 1928. He was an internationally respected scientist and a beloved mentor to many at the Cardiovascular Pulmonary Laboratory of the University of Colorado in Denver. He died in Colorado, 15th September 2004.

A Million Leaves

Who can tell, when
the first leaf falls,
how many more will follow.

Who knows, as the
cold wind blows,
how many fields lie fallow.

We come from the
same tree and return
to the dark forest floor.

Whether high above
or in the soil beneath,
we nourish and support.

Written after a million COVID-19 deaths in the USA.

Memini Ergo Sum

Memory is what makes us human,
allows the violinist to inscribe a phrase,
the teacher to entrance her class,
the chef to seduce the palate.

When the mother does not know her child,
the priest the words of the communion,
then the bell has no striker, no sound,
is not a bell.

Memini ergo sum: I remember, therefore I am.
The title is my adaptation of the famous quotation
of the French philosopher, Rene' Descartes (1596–1650),
"cogito ergo sum," I think, therefore I am.

I Knew a Man

Doubtless he would say
the soul survives the body;
that after death some
vestige will remain.
Where dwells his soul, now
that strokes destroyed his mind
and yet his body lives?

When he could no more discuss
the philosophy of Kant,
did his soul depart?

It's a Dog's Life

A squirrel ran beside him,
he didn't even stir.
I'm old but not that stupid,
last week he barked at Her.

Sometimes there is nobody
to open up the door.
He doesn't know the diff'rence
'tween the garden and the floor.

Since They cured dog cancer,
put statins in our bowl,
there are old dogs all over
who do not know a soul.

If we do not know our Owner,
can't shuffle to the fire,
if They know that life is over
and a whistle can't inspire,

when They can no longer keep you
and the block is in the shed,
if you know your number's calling,
send the tabby cat instead.

Written during the Healthcare debate, 2010;
thoughts on End of Life Choices and Death Panels.

The Will of the Living

Two hundred thousand years ago
he couldn't fight off the hyenas,
so his children escaped with their children,
his death a fortunate distraction.

One hundred thousand years ago
the old man of forty years
could no longer ford the river,
so they left him sitting under the tree,
as his father before him.

Ten thousand years ago
the oldest of the tribe fell,
too slow to hunt, though still cunning,
his eyes failing, his stomach empty,
they buried him beneath a cairn of rocks.

One thousand years ago
the last rites recited,
the grandfather died,
his family around him,
the priests processed, promising eternal life.

Today, he lies alone
absent in mind, minded by monitors
and when the alarm sounds, they rush
to drag him back to the land of the living,
to which he was already dead.

Television-Induced Attention Deficit (TVAD)

To think, or not to think…
That is the question. Whether
'tis easier in the mind
to watch the channels change,
a consummation devoutly to be wisht,
or plagiarize a line to feed a verse.

With apologies to Prince Hamlet.

Publish or Perish

Thoughts thought
are not thought
to be thought
unless published.

Published thought
may be thought
less thoughtful
than the thinker
thought.

Published thought
does not make
the thinker
a poet or a sage.

Previously published in the Minnesota Medical Journal.

Icarus, the Scientist

We grope forward in the dark,

then, like moths, perceive the light,

soar up in riotous flight but

scorched, fall back into the night.

Icarus Statue

Section 3

Religion and Politics

Belief. What you believe may be different from what I believe. Yet, precisely because a belief is just that, a belief, one cannot be proven against another. For thousands of years, humans believed that they should pay homage to the Sun-God, or the Moon-God, or both. Few do so today. The conflicts seeded in belief, between individuals and between nations, illustrate the importance of separating facts from beliefs.

"Whatever may be our wishes, our inclinations, or the dictates of our passion, they cannot alter the state of facts and evidence."

John Adams (Second US President)

"The spirit of liberty is the spirit which is not too sure that it is right."

US Judge Learned Hand

"Everyone is entitled to his own opinion, but not to his own facts."

Daniel Patrick Moynihan

"The personal and the political cannot be separated, but are entwined in a double helix model."

Joan Didion. Quoted by Annie Correal in the New York Times—30th May 2018.

"Politics be King's games and for the most part played upon the scaffold."

Sir Thomas Moore.

"One should, for example, be able to see that things are hopeless and yet be determined to make them otherwise."

F. Scott Fitzgerald.

Which True Religion?

God has no favorites among babies.
Children live in the faith of their mothers.
Shinto, Shiite, Sunni, Sikh.
They marry in the church of their fathers.
They lie in the soil of their homelands,
buried in the rites that sustained them.
Baptist, Buddhist, Lutheran, Jew,
each belief true as another,
each god, just as the next.

Before Moses climbed the Mount,
or Jesus rowed on Galilee,
who wrought salvation then?
Delphic oracle and Druid glade
each spoke the Truth
for a people and a time.

Before His Time

Cremated and buried
in a nook at Newgrange,
lit by the rising sun
at the Winter solstice,

how could I know
the risen Christ,
being dead three thousand
years before his birth.

Where is my sin
if I worshipped the sun
and never knew the son
of God?

On visiting the great burial mound at Newgrange, Boyne Valley, Ireland built around 3,200BC (pre-dating the pyramids of Giza in Egypt).
Homo sapiens has been in existence for over 300,000 years.

Parallel Universes

One listened to the voices around him
and shot the governor,
in Islamabad.
They say he is inspired.

Another listened to the voices within his head
and shot a congresswoman,
in Tucson, Arizona.
We say he is insane.

One is arguably sane
in a deranged society;
the other palpably mad
in a partly rational world.

Salman Taseer, Governor of Punjab, was assassinated because of his opposition to Pakistan's blasphemy laws.
4th January 2011

Congresswoman Gabrielle D Giffords was shot in Tucson.
8th January 2011

Pro-Choice

Montague or Capulet,
Mormon or Catholic,
Rangers or Celtic,
Capitalist, Communist,
Gay, straight?
Choose, choose one!

Republican, Democrat
Wahhabi or Christian,
Atheist or Hasidic Jew,
Turban or burqa,
Boshi or kippah?
Choose, choose now!

I choose to believe
That no one, no group
Knows the Truth,
And that knowledge,
That I do not know,
Makes me free.

Divine Providence

The albino squirrel is special.
He doesn't know why, but
each morning, when he appears,
I put out a handful of seed.

The grey squirrels, larger
and more numerous,
are not allowed to forage
in his domain.

The Puritans knew that they
were special, chosen by God;
preferred over Catholics.
So it is with Shia and Sunni,
Jew and Gentile.

Now it makes sense:
the God we imagine
is not just, but just
as capricious as I.

Fundamental Truths

Truth can be an equation
provable to a finite degree of certainty,
or it may be "perceived",
certain only to that individual.

I may believe, because I do not know,
but if I know, there is no doubt,
no need for revelation.
A proven fact requires no faith.

Belief can be confused with knowledge
but two men's beliefs may be opposed.
Unquestioned faith may end in strife,
and who can say which one is right.

Reflective Validation

One person with bizarre beliefs
is delusional.
A small group with such beliefs
is a cult.
A large group espousing such beliefs
is a religion.
If most people share these beliefs,
then those who do not, are atheists,
and clearly are deluded.

I Will Convert You from Peanuts to Almonds

They inform me that you
do not adore the Almond.
All my people rejoice in
the essence of the Almond.

Every summer eve, my father
would ascend to the stall
in the high casbah
to hear the Almond seller's call.

They say, you and your kind
are peanut eaters. If you
had not tasted the Almond;
if I did not know, you knew,

you could be forgiven.
But you reject the Almond
and when the peanut lands are barren
you will reap a bitter harvest.

Musings on a simple comment. I overheard a Turkish friend say the title line to a colleague.

Not Second Nature

Crows, strutting ungainly,
lift from the damp grass,
rise on urgent wings and
fly joyous in the wind
above the sodden land.

What benighted crow,
confused and blown off course
would stall, wings flailing,
and fall into the dark waves
or densely wooded hill?

Our little plane struggles
into the turbulent sky,
lurches from cloud to cloud,
while fearful passengers
cross themselves. Ave, Ave, Ave.

So, by grace, we land
And taxi to the gate.

The captain stands, his head
suffused by cockpit light.
Thank you, Father.

Church and State

God does not issue edicts,
publish bulletins, declare his mind.
Many claim to speak for God,
so many and so much at odds
that some may be deluded.

If some are right,
how might we know?
Does God rejoice
in the burning bush,
or in the still small voice?

Hanging is not the work of an
omnipotent, beneficent God
but of old and impotent men,
whose hold on temporal power
is hidden 'neath a cloak of faith.

Arash Rahmanipour did not betray his God.
If God abandoned him,
I cannot tell, but this I know,

if righteous revelation be the Law,
then man is God and God, fallible.

Arash Rahmanipour, 19 years, was executed, 28th January 2010, in Iran, on charges of waging war against God (Moharebeh).

In the Likeness of Man

If I who made you did not exist,
you would have conjured me,
to comfort you in the darkness,
in fear of the known and unknown.

To be insignificant,
fluke of random evolution,
sentient but inconsequential,
would be intolerable.

My name and image,
majesty and judgement seat,
omniscience and omnipotence,
stem from your conceit.

Act of God, March 2011

In the corner of my greenhouse
there is a colony of industrious ants.
Yesterday I walked on the bricks
beside their nest, each step
crumbling the dry earth.

I turned on the water to fill
the barrel and was distracted
by the antics of warring squirrels
on a distant tree, each fighting
for dominance and territory.

The skirmish over, I saw the water
cascading down the barrel,
flooding over the bricks and soil,
washing ants and eggs down the drain.
How careless of me.

"Act of God, March 2011" refers to the tsunami in Japan and wars in Libya/Yemen etc.

Charles I, the Thirtieth of January, 1648

The execution day dawned fair.
The King walked briskly
through the banqueting hall,
where he had often dined before,
out the window to the scaffold.
The murmur of the crowd grew loud.

The bishop took the royal cloak and said,
"There is but one stage more; it will
soon carry you a very great way; to the
prize you hasten to, a crown of glory."
The King replied, "I go from a corruptible
to an incorruptible crown."

When the blade fell and the axeman
lifted up his head and flourished it aloft,
did the Heavens open and a choir of angels
raise the martyr to their host, were
Laud and Strafford there to greet their King, or
was the last dim sight, of blood beneath the block?

Epilogue. The First of April, 1813

The body of King Charles was exhumed.
Did he look down upon a monarchy restored
and laugh in righteous vindication,
or would he have exchanged the tarnished crown for life,
had he but known that earth is all we are?

Dissonance

If the program says Mozart
but the winds play Wagner
and the second violins
shriek dissent,
is the conductor to blame?

Written when the Obama Affordable Care Act was being debated.

Volatility

Despite the cold, the sun
feels warm upon my back.
The feeder's full and on the ground
the small-cap juncos peck.
Should I spread the wealth,
kick sunflower seed below?
But no, emerging markets urge
the flight to Southern climes.

Yet wait, there's thistle seed
awasting and dividends to
pluck before we fly.
Perhaps a short diversion North
in search of golden grains?
The NASDAQ and the sun's still high,
why have the faint-hearts fled?
The high-flying indices plunge down;
their talons tear my nest apart.

Israeli Election, St Patrick's Day, 17th March 2015

One state, two states?
Not even St. Patrick can
exorcise these snakes.

Haiku.

Judgment of Solomon

Would that the wisdom of Solomon
were wrought in the halls of Congress.
But no, rather than sacrifice
one iota of partisan advantage,
both parties would rather
the country was torn in two.

Choices

If there is a God
nothing else matters.
If there is no God
everything matters.

She will nurture
Her creation,
care for Her children,
provide the hereafter.

Alternatively,
there is only one world,
your life is your own,
eternity is now.

J'Accuse

Were You there
when my uncle was sold
into slavery,
when my mother knelt
in the gas chamber,
when the tsunami swept
over my head?
Were You there
when AIDS despoiled
my sister?

Though omniscient, You choose
not to know;
though omnipotent,
not to act;
infallible, yet
so flawed.
It would be easier
to believe
that You
do not
exist.

Raptured

This morning I looked in the mirror
but no-one looked back at me.
When I turned around to my bed,
I was still there but ever so still.

Called to my wife who ignored me,
to the dog who declined to go walk.
On my desk was a memo, "Gone to talk
with the fellow upstairs. Back after tea."

Mortality

A wisp of cloud separates
from the tumultuous mass,
dissipates, and the clear blue sky
betrays no trace that it
was ever there.

Sudden Cardiac Arrest

Still dressed in Summer's green,
no sudden chill or clouded brow,
no southern flight of geese,
gave warning of the early Fall,
foretold the waking of the dead.

The last line refers to the tradition in country areas in Ireland—of celebrating the memory of the deceased, often with an open coffin.

Irish Famine Sculpture

The sculpture of a gaunt hand reaching from the ground is called "The Famine", an emotional subject for any Irishman.

Section 4

Aging, Love and Family

Family. Choose your parents wisely. The impossibility of that advice is self-evident. However, it illustrates the fact that much of what we are, we enjoy, or endure, is the product of our genetics and early upbringing.

In terms of stereotypes that have suffered discrimination, theoretically you could be "black, Irish, and a Jew". We deserve no credit if we are lucky enough to be born into a strong supportive family, or blame, if the opposite is true. Nobel or know-nothing, who you are today is largely an accident of birth. What do you think?

Gene Pool

Smart? She was smart,
never lost at Scrabble,
remembered relatives of
neighbors, dead for decades,
chemical formulae, and forms
of etiquette, all stacked
in the library of her mind.

Later, it seemed, she
could no longer find
the right shelf. Rummaged
around to recall those
who had eaten at her table
the previous night.
My Mother had…what's his name?
You know…that …
that disease.

Previously published in the Minnesota Medical Journal.

Paddy

The last sail is furled,
the ball is down the line,
the brimming glass now empty,
but you will find him at the end
of every rainbow in the County Donegal.

For my cousin, Paddy Moss, sailor, rugby scrum-half and lover of life:
(16th December 1933 – 25th May 2011)

Simplicity

Mooney stood here 150 years ago.
He came from Old Ireland
bringing new life to the New World:
poor but rich in determination,
sick but strong in his faith,
simple but blessed in simplicity.
Now we live on his lake,
rich but impoverished by doubt,
strong but bound by fears,
learnèd but confused by knowledge.

Oh, to step boldly into the past.

We have lived on a hill overlooking Mooney Lake for over 40 years.

Alzheimer's

A human
Infliction?
Inflection?
Affliction!
Well anyway,
it wouldn't
happen to
a dog.

He
could not
communicate
his failure
to remember.
Each tree trunk
still provides
the Twitter
of the evening
past.

Would a rose
smell as sweet
if the nose
had lost
its memory?

Restraint

A thought may ring around
the hollow of my skull
but if it be unheard
then it can do no harm.

A thought is not a bird
and though it cries,
it need not be set free
to fly from mind to mind
and rend the troubled air.

Anno Domini

Fifty years past,
we met
by a pool.
You were
effervescent,
lithe,
warm.

The pool is older now,
cracks in the concrete,
chips in the tiles,
rust on the steps
but the water, is hot.

Elizabeth

Though all are convinced
that education is elitist,
health care is not a right
and that the poor are idle,

in the sun-besotted field
there is one sunflower
which resolutely turns her face
towards the stars.

La Mort D'Amour

Some men die in their sleep,
others die in battle,
some sink into the deep
but I, I live for you.

Some men pray for long life,
many to feel no pain,
all desire to stay strong
but me, my strength is you.

When at last you falter,
the joy fades from your eyes,
when Autumn turns to Winter,
then happily I die.

If You Have These

The smell of turf smoke,
roar of Atlantic rollers,
the splash of purple heather,
blaze of orange montbretia,
the dark promise of blackberries,
the crackle of grasshoppers,
keening of a gull
or rasp of the crows,
the hand of a man
who knew your father,
the laughter of friends,
the silence of the full moon,
the stone on which
my brothers sat,

I have no more to give.

For our son, Fergus, in the coming times.

The Cloth of Life

Though the weave be rough and edges frayed
may the fiber of your life be full of color.
Without the prompting of a priest or prelate
may you know the heft of right and wrong.
As your spirit soars above the tumult of the river
may the sunlight sparkle on the waves.
When you walk among the dapple of the woodland,
painted from the palette of your Mother's love,
may nothing now be left unsaid between you
for all she ever gave you, is your soul.

For our son, Conor.

Not to Know

At night the sheriff came again.
"No, nothing. Nothing new."

How can I not know
if my heart does not beat,
if my lungs do not breathe,
if my limbs are torn apart?
How can a twin not know
when the mirror breaks?

Know nothing. Never. Night.

Written for my friend at the time his wife was lost in the Rockies and never found.

Not to Know Sculpture

Section 5

History and Remembrance

"The only thing necessary for the triumph of evil is for good men to do nothing."

Edmund Burke

"We cannot defend freedom abroad by deserting it at home."

Edward R. Murrow

"The moral test of government is how that government treats those who are in the dawn of life, the children; and those who are in the twilight of life, the elderly; and those who are in the shadows of life, the sick, the needy and the handicapped."

Hubert Humphrey

"Poetry is speech at its most personal."

W. H. Auden

"Those Who fail to Learn from History Are..."

Empty shoes above the Danube,
shoes of Jews who fell below.
But where are the boots, the memory,
of those who struck the fatal blow.

Each had a Mother and friends
like those who fell in the water.
Unless the seed of hate is plucked
from the mind, history will recur.

Written after seeing the bronze shoes on the quay above the Danube in Budapest; a memorial to those children, women and men who were killed there in 1945 and whose bodies fell in the river.
The title..." doomed to repeat it" is ascribed to Sir Winston Churchill.

A Fisher of Men

Baton raised;
Rod poised;
Crowd hushed.

A single note, barely perceptible;
The line shimmers out;
The president smiles.

The sound floats in the air;
Fly dances on the water;
"We here in the heartland…"

The ear transfixed;
The line taut;
"Safe from terror…"

The mind enthralled;
The hook set;
"No draft. No new taxes."

The opus over;
The net is full;
Mission accomplished.

George W. Bush (May 2003)
As conductor of an orchestra, or as a fly fisherman with rod in hand.

Iraqi Requiem

It's raining in Baghdad. Drops in the dusty street,
blood bright in the air, mingles with the call to prayer.
Lives needlessly lost. Foes recklessly forged.
Kyrie eleison.

No WMD, just mass deception,
no Sadam, Osama terror connection;
just blood for oil, brave lives for spoil.
Christe eleison.

Had George seen war in Vietnam,
Tom would live to see his son,
Dick would see and Harry walk.
Kyrie eleison.

At the last trump there is a place set by
for those who cannot see, or talk, or cry
and for those who see and hear but do not care.

Quantus tremor est futurus
Quando Judex est venturus.

Written at the end of the first year of the Iraq war.
Kyrie eleison: *Lord have mercy*
Christe eleison: *Christ have mercy*
Words from the Latin mass.
Quantus tremor…
What fear there will be
When the Judge will come.
From *Verdi's Requiem*.

Evasion

War without Cause,
War without Cost,
Words without Conscience,
Flags without Valor,
Bravado without Service,
Promises without Shame,
Tears without Pain,
Spin without Substance,
Death without Gain,
Power without Responsibility.

Written back in 2nd May 2005, relating to the Bush administration's rhetoric in support of the war in Iraq and over 1000 American deaths.

Iraqi Bookends

If Christ only knew
how His name,
twisted on a tongue,
could impale minds
to justify a war;
Dulce et decorum est.

Basra, Falujah,
Sheik, and Mullah,
Sunni, Sufi,
Home town boy;
Pro patria mori.

Three days remorse
would have kept
the stone in place;
Pro mundo mori

4th April 2005
Dulce et decorum est pro patria mori: It is sweet and proper to die for your country.
Pro mundo mori: to die for the world.

Contraconception

He cannot conceive
the pain of three thousand deaths,
or thirty thousand;
the consequence of melting ice
or creep of sterile sand;
the impact of unwanted birth;
the vice of poverty
or the grip of vice.
Though born again
he cannot conceive.

George W. Bush.
Written at the beginning of 2007, when the deaths of US forces in Iraq reached 3,000.

Dunsinane DC

An adequate actor,
he knows his part.
He learns his lines,
performs before millions,
denounces his enemies,
declaims against imagined threats,
consults with ethereal powers,
succors his friends and allies.

But then 3,000 Banquos rise,
the branches fall in Birnam Wood;
we know which part he plays
but where's MacDuff?

Written in response to an Op-Ed in the New York Times by Bob Herbert deploring Mr. Bush's failure to understand what he has wrought in Iraq and calling for politicians with courage. At that point in the war over 3,000 Americans had died in Iraq.

The Defense Lobbyist

He makes a sortie late in the morning,
cajoling in Cannon, a recce in Rayburn,
returns safely to his base on K Street
in time for the lunchtime libation.

Young men return through Dover;
grief returns to the heartland.

Cannon and Rayburn are congressional office buildings.
A "recce" is an abbreviation for a reconnaissance.
Coffins of servicemen from overseas are flown into
Dover air base.

Hindsight 2020

So successful, the candidate,
we thought our little boats
would rise with his, not be flooded
in his wake.

An affable man, the nominee,
so when he failed to tell the truth
we assumed he wasn't serious,
but he was.

He was Christian, the elected,
so we knew he would support the poor,
care for the sick, comfort the bereaved,
but he doesn't.

Tolerant of intolerance, the President,
exploits a rising tide of ignorance,
denounces enemies of the state and
sends them to our gulag
in Guantanamo.

Written in 2007.

Let's Make Truth Great Again

Humpty Trumpty sat on a virtual wall,
Humpty Trumpty had a magnificent fall.
All the GOP horses and all the GOP men
Couldn't put Trumpty together again.

Humpty Trumpty believed in "truthism",
This is a concept something like nudism.
The President has no clothes, but like VP Pence,
Half the country can't tell the difference.

With apologies to all who value the integrity of nursery stories.

Rule(~~s~~)r of the Road

On Mondays, I stop at the Stop signs,
because I am the “Law and Order” Leader.

On Tuesdays, I ignore the stop signs,
because they limit my freedom of choice.

On Wednesdays, I respect the Stop signs,
because they were made by American workers.

On Thursdays, I flout the stop signs,
because they are excessive government regulation.

On Fridays, I pause at the Stop signs,
because Ivanka is in the front seat.

On Saturdays, I flatten the stop signs,
because they are enforced by so-called judges.

On Sundays, I obey the Stop signs,
because only (erase those that do not apply)

illegal immigrants,
godless elite liberals,
the lying news media,
treasonous NSA agents
would do otherwise.

False Prophets

11th November 1918
The guns fell silent
but in the dark morass of defeat,
the bitter seeds of hatred and despair
germinated, flourished, and
tended by a demagogue,
in time, shut out the sun.

11th August 2016
Now a global conflict
fought with robots and icons
determines who shall prosper.
The siren voice returns,
amplified by the clashing rocks
of ignorance and anger.
The midday sun grows dim.

11th November 1918 was Armistice Day, the end of World War I.
8th November 2016 was Election Day in the USA.

Conservative Mantra

Rather deplore abortion,
than promote contraception;
grieve over the dead, than
outlaw the guns that killed them.

Rather wage war than negotiate,
whether at home or abroad;
rather trust in what you believe,
than in science-based fact;
rather incarcerate the father,
than teach the child.

Shadows Etch the Dial

Around the sundial on the lawn
twelve standard roses stood erect
and one by one declared the hours.
Beyond the pane our brother slept,
each strident breath, each beat, a gift.

Sunrise marked the waking hour but
clouds conspired to seize the light;
the unrequited heart abruptly ceased.
Rain gathered on the dial,
the hours lost in reflection.

John Fergus Weir—13th May 1937 – 14th November1959
My brother.

Older Brother

Not Father but friend,
not Mother but mentor,
not parent but peer,
not twin but tutor.

Thanks to your training
our parents had sound hands,
no longer terrified novices
facing imperious demands.

The first to live,
the first to canter
past the finishing post,
always the leader.

The Nature of Nature

When a tornado wrenched our woods,
it was the strongest of trees that fell.
Now we have lost a great oak,
whose branches shielded and shaded us all.
It is the cycle of Nature.

The canopy of our lives
is torn asunder.

Venkat, My Friend

When my father died,
my mother became my father too.
When my mother died,
everything that they
have taught me, is them.
I am them to my children,
my friends and the world.
While I am alive,
they live.

Ready or Not

I go ahead,
down by the lake,
where the white squirrel nests
and the wood-ducks dive
I will be waiting.

In early Spring,
when the ice crackles
on the frozen shore,
you will hear my voice
when the wild geese call.

Nihil Verius

Fire will melt ice
and ice will quench fire.
Truth and falsehood
cannot coexist.

Nihil verius is our Weir family motto. Translated from the Latin it means, "Nothing More True".

In Memoriam

George Edward Ffrench,
Royal Air Force

Loyal, where loyalty is deemed a crime,
He scorned the baseness of the lesser breed
Who snatch advantage from the Empire's need
Contriving treason in this anxious time.
Fresh come from school and field, with faith sublime
His young heroic soul blazed forth in deed;
Riding the perilous air at fearful speed
He rushed to meet his fate in early prime.
"The everlasting arms are underneath"
He wrote: and confidently we believe
For him and his compeers there is no death!
Unseen, the arms are ready to receive;
And when the plane is shattered past reprieve
Peace falls benign from battle's fiery breath.

The Rev. G. E. Ffrench.

George Edward Ffrench was my Mother's oldest brother.

He was killed in France, May 23rd, 1918, aged 18, a second lieutenant in the Royal Air Force. He is buried in the Pernes British Cemetery, Pas de Calais, France.

This poem for my uncle was written in his honor by his uncle; The Rev. G. E. Ffrench, a Church of Ireland minister. The poem, "An Irish Airman Foresees his Death" by William Butler Yeats, written in 1918 but published in 1919, has echoes of this poem.

Reading the Ffrench poem, it is striking how much has changed and yet how much stays the same from one generation to the next. What do you think?